Publié la première fois par Secret Quay Media 2015

Droit d'auteur M. Gail Daldy 2013 - 2017

Ce qui arrive par chance avec Chance | ISBN 978-0-9947957-2-4

Série Apprendre avec Chance: Pour commander un exemplaire du livre, écrire à _orders@learnbychancebooks.com_ ou composer le 1-604-947-9283

Consultez notre site à www.learnbychancebooks.com

Directeur artistique: Jason Bamford | Bamford Design | www.bamforddesign.com

Photographies de Gail Daldy

Un remerciement spécial à tous ceux qui ont contribués à la traduction ainsi qu' à Mark Johnston pour toute son aide.

Un court commentaire au sujet de cette traduction: "Chance" est le nom de mon garçon, mais cela signifie aussi .... Que les photos ont été prises par hazard.

Publié par:
Secret Quay Media Inc.
Box 91194
West Vancouver, British Columbia, Canada
V7V 3N6

www.secretquaymedia.com

Imprimé aux É.-U.

First published by Secret Quay Media Inc. 2015

Copyright © M. Gail Daldy 2013 - 2017

Things That Happen By Chance | ISBN 978-0-9947957-2-4

Learn By Chance book series: To order a copy of the book email _orders@learnbychancebooks.com_, or call 1-604-947-9283

Visit us online at www.learnbychancebooks.com

Creative Director: Jason Bamford | Bamford Design | www.bamforddesign.com

Photographs by Gail Daldy

A special thank you to all of those who contributed to the translation and, to Mark Johnston for all of his help.

A note on the translation: "Chance" is the name of my son, but it also means .... the pictures were taken by chance.

Published By:
Secret Quay Media Inc.
Box 91194
West Vancouver, British Columbia, Canada
V7V 3N6

www.secretquaymedia.com

Printed in USA

Ce qui arrive par chance avec Chance

En feuillettant parmi les photos de notre fils Chance, j'ai instantanément été transportée au moment de sa tendre enfance. En guise de cadeau de fin d'études secondaires, je me suis dit que ce serait amusant de rassembler tous ces clichés pris au hasard et d'en faire un petit livre.

Les caractères typographiques furent créés à partir de ses premiers écrits au niveau primaire. Mon souhait était de l'amener à réfléchir à son enfance et à ses moments spéciaux pour qu'il puisse partager ces leçons quotidiennes apprises durant sa jeunesse avec ses propres enfants. Après tout, ce sont ces moments-là qui ont fait de lui la personne qui existe aujourd'hui.

J'espère que vous profiterez du livre avec vos petits lecteurs et que vous discuterez, en souriant, de ces petits moments de la vie quotidienne qui leur enseigneront des leçons essentielles.

Un remerciement spécial
J'aimerais remercier mes parents, qui m'ont fait découvrir ces petits moments précieux de la vie quotidienne.

What Happened By Chance

While looking through some photographs of our son Chance growing up they instantly took me back in time to his early childhood. As my gift to him upon graduating high school I thought it would be fun to put together a collection of these chance snapshots into a little book.

The type face is actually created from some of his earliest hand writing in primary school. My hope was that he would be able to reflect back on his childhood and some of the special moments and share these everyday life lessons that he had learned as a child with his own children. It was these moments after all that made him into the person he has grown up to be.

Hopefully you can enjoy the book with your own little readers and with a smile talk about the simple things in life that teach them so much.

A Special Thanks
I'd like to thank my parents for making me aware of these little things in life.

www.learnbychancebooks.com

À Chance:

Pour m'offrir le bonheur ultime d'une
maman - celui de te voir t'épanouir.

To Chance:

For affording me a mother's ultimate
pleasure of watching you become *you.*

Ce qui arrive par chance avec Chance

Things That Happen By Chance

Partager des leçons simples de la vie quotidienne avec des enfants de partout

Sharing simple life lessons with children everywhere

La vie est remplie
de petites surprises

Life is always filled
with little surprises

vaer sa snill   budakamnida   Kirpa Karke   varog   min fa lika

kripya   alstublieft   per favore   s'il vous plait   Kerem

tolong   e'olu olu   fadlam   please   parakalo

bud'laska   molim

prosze   kudasai   pozalujsta   snalla   asseblief

xin   lotfan   por favor   bitte   ake

le do thoil

bevekshah   Kor   doya Kore   mghoi   os gwelwch yn dda

4

Si tu demandes quelque chose,
souviens-toi toujours de dire
s'il-vous-plaît

When you are asking
for something always
remember to say please

Si quelqu'un t'aide,
souviens-toi de sourire et
de dire merci

When someone helps you
always remember to smile
and say thank you

dhonnobad   mahalo   moteshakkeram   go raibh maith agat   mghoi

kiitos   dankie   hvala lepo   diolch   arigatou   multumesc

shukran   Xin cam on   diakuju   obrigato   grazie   tanvad

efharisto   spasibo

xiexie

danku   merci   thank you   terima kasih   dziekuje

todah   tesekkur   ngiyabonga   danke

tack   gracias   mersi   Koszonom

mahadsanid   takk   Kamsahamnida   shukriya   khawp khun

Si tu mâches de la gomme,
souviens-toi de trois choses :
1. Garde-la dans ta bouche
2. Ne l'avale pas
3. Ne la mets jamais dans tes cheveux

If you chew gum
remember 3 things :
1. keep it in your mouth
2. Don't swallow it
3. Never put it in your hair

Lorsqu'il y a une tâche
à faire, cela t'aidera de penser
à un plan d'action

When there is a job
to be done it helps to
plan your attack

Et d'y tenir bon

And stick to it

13

Jusqu'au bout

Until the very end

Non,
je ne pense pas avoir mangé
des petites "grignotines au fromage

NO
I don't think I ate
any cheesies

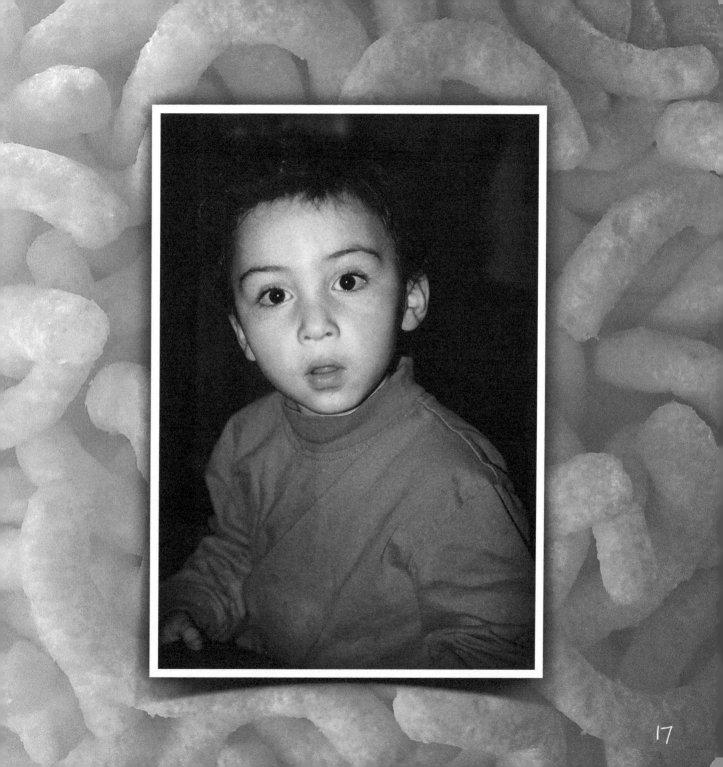

C'est très amusant
de nourrir les oiseaux
et les canards

Feeding the
birds and ducks
is lots of fun

Mais n'oublie pas
de refermer la porte
de la clôture derrière toi

But don't forget
to close
the gate

Parfois, tu peux manger
trop de gâteau
au chocolat

you can eat
too much
chocolate cake

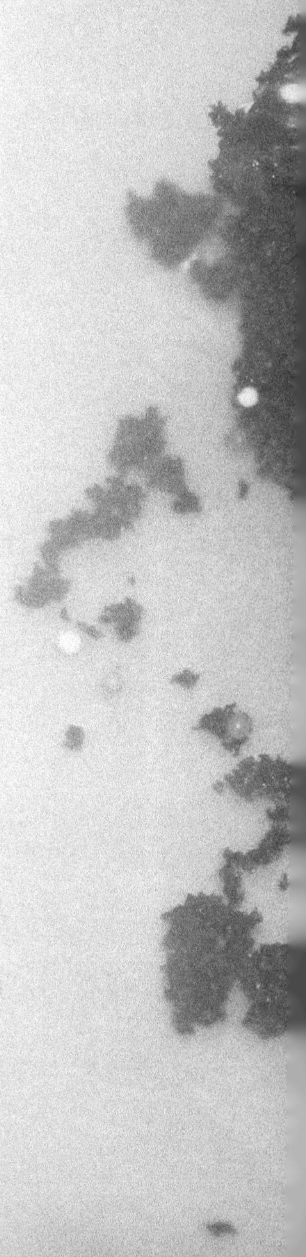

23

Brosse tes dents à tous
les jours pour qu'elles restent
propres et saines

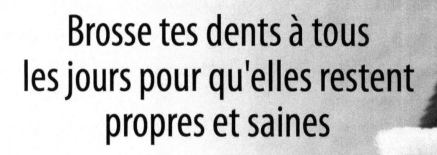

Be sure to brush your
teeth every day to keep
them clean and healthy

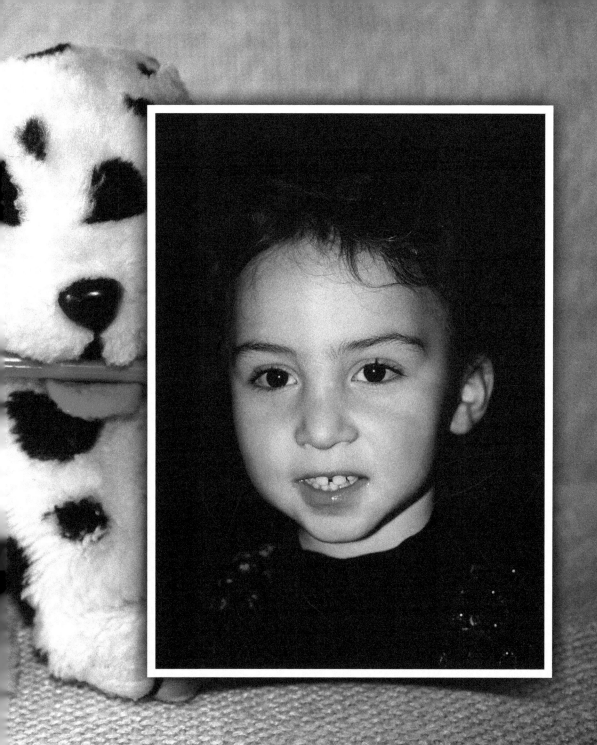

25

Ne mets jamais
les doigts
dans ton nez

Always keep your
fingers on the
outside of your nose

Si tu es indécis
ou incertain au sujet
de quelque chose

If there is
something you are
not sure about

29

Et si quelqu'un ou quelque
chose te rend mal à l'aise,
parles-en tout de suite
à un adulte

And someone or something
makes you feel not right
inside be sure to tell
a grown up right away

Si tu as des gaz
ou des petites
"pétarades souterraines",
fais-le en privé

Wind and thunder
from down under
should be done
in private

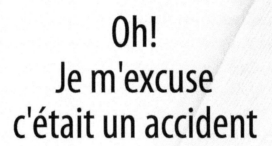

Oh!
Je m'excuse
c'était un accident

I'm sorry
it was an
accident

C'est rigolo
d'apprendre à
faire des biscuits

It's fun learning
how to
bake cookies

Fais attention
de bien
mélanger tous
les ingrédients

Make sure
you mix all of the
ingredients together
really good

39

N'oublie jamais
de te laver
les mains avant
de commencer

And always remember
to wash your hands
before
you start

Si un ami
a besoin
de te parler,

When a friend
needs someone
to talk to

43

Essaie
toujours de bien
l'écouter

Always try
to be a
good listener

45

Ne mange jamais,
jamais de neige
qui n'est pas
fraîchement tombée

Never never
ever ever
eat
yellow snow

Parfois, il y a des gens
qui racontent des histoires
qui ne sont pas toujours vraies

Sometimes
people tell stories
that are not true

49

Sois certain de
toujours raconter des
histoires qui sont vraies

Make sure you
tell stories
that are true

C'est bon de
sentir le vent
dans ses cheveux

It's fun to feel the
wind blow through
your hair

et le sable
entre ses orteils

and the sand wiggle
between your toes

Si tu es gentil,
tu te feras
plusieurs d'amis

Being nice makes
all kinds of
friends

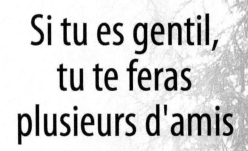

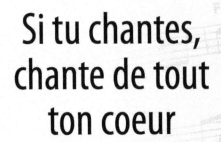

Si tu chantes,
chante de tout
ton coeur

When you sing,
sing with all
your heart

59

À chaque fois
que tu en as
la chance, danse

whenever you get
the chance
just dance

Prends toujours
le temps de
sentir les fleurs

Always take the
time to stop
and smell the flowers

Merci d'avoir lu mon petit livre
et de m'avoir permis de partager
avec vous ces quelques leçons de la
vie de tous les jours avec moi
(par chance et avec Chance)

Thank you for reading my
little book and letting me
share some of my real
life lessons with you
by Chance

À propos de l'auteure

Gail Daldy est née à Chilliwack en Colombie-Britannique, sur la côte Ouest du Canada. Elle s'est plus tard installée à Bowen Island, une île voisine de Vancouver. Jeune femme, elle a beaucoup voyagé, découvrant ainsi les différentes cultures et le quotidien de plusieurs pays.

C'est à ce moment qu'elle a réalisé que tous les enfants du monde entier se ressemblent et qu'ils peuvent apprendre les uns des autres les petites choses quotidiennes qui les entourent. Selon elle, cette collection de photos de Chance capte plusieurs de ces leçons quotidiennes et les illustre d'une manière facile à comprendre.

About the Author

Gail Daldy was born in Chilliwack, British Columbia on the west coast of Canada before settling on Bowen Island which is just off the Vancouver mainland. As a young woman she travelled extensively experiencing different cultures and everyday living in numerous countries.

From this she realized children are similar the world over and can learn from each other and the simple things that surround them. She believes this collection of chance photographs captures many of these everyday life lessons and illustrates them in an easy to understand way.

Ce livre est le premier de la série Apprendre avec Chance
This is the first book of the Learn by Chance series.

"Kids will really relate to the photos in this book, and be both inspired and amused." - **Temple Grandin, Author,** *Thinking in Pictures*

"These masterful photographs with entertaining and clever text makes "Things That Happen By Chance" a perfect book to impart useful knowledge to a young child and start wonderful conversations." - **Tom Best, Executive Director,** *First Book Canada*

"A delightful addition to our Reach Out and Read program!"
- **Dr. Laurie Green,** *Reach Out and Read Canada*

Things That Happen By Chance

To say "A picture is worth 1000 words" seems so cliché while at the same time appropriate in pointing out the obvious in this little book of Chance.

As seen through the eyes of one little boy a growing visual interactive experience of a child learning simple life lessons that can be shared with children all over the world.

Seeing and reading about his adventures as they happen creates a great conversation opener for parents giving them an opportunity to talk about similar enjoyable moments and lessons learned with their own children.

GAIL DALDY

Taking a closer look at the little things in life

learnbychancebooks.com

ISBN 978-0-9947957-2-4

$18.95 USD | for ages 2 & up

ISBN 978-0-9947957-2-4

CPSIA information can be obtained
at www.ICGtesting.com
Printed in the USA
LVHW05s2121230418
574606LV00004B/5/P